HMH |  into Reading™

Writer's Notebook

GRADE 5

Printed in the U.S.A.

ISBN   978-1-328-47013-3

12 13 14 15 16   2677   26 25 24 23 22

4500852355   A B C D E F G

Grade
5

Contents

MODULE 1: Expository Essay

MODULE 2: Story

MODULE 3: Persuasive Essay

MODULE 4: Letter

MODULE 5: Editorial

MODULE 6: Personal Narrative

MODULE 7: Research Report

MODULE 8: Lyric Poem

MODULE 9: Imaginative Story

MODULE 10: Letter to the Editor

MODULE 11: Realistic Story

MODULE 12: Narrative Poem

Word Bank

As you listen to *Girls Think of Everything*, write interesting words about inventors or inventions. You can use this Word Bank as a resource as you draft and revise your writing.

Name _____

Expository Essay Rubric

Use this rubric to develop and revise your draft expository essay. Ask yourself if each statement in the rubric describes your essay. Stretch to score a 4 in each category!

Score	Organization	Ideas & Support	Conventions
4	My writing is organized and includes an introduction, transitions, and a conclusion.	My writing develops one central idea with specific details.	• My writing uses a variety of sentence structures. • My writing includes proper grammar, spelling, capitalization, and punctuation.
3	My ideas are mostly organized. I have an introduction, a conclusion, and some transitions.	My writing mostly develops one central idea with specific details.	• My writing uses some variety in sentence structures. • My writing has a few errors in grammar, spelling, capitalization or punctuation.
2	Few ideas are organized. I may be missing an introduction, conclusion, or transitions.	My writing hardly develops a central idea. It does not have enough details.	• Few sentences are varied. • My writing has some errors in grammar, usage, capitalization, and spelling.
1	My ideas are not organized. My writing is missing an introduction, transitions, and a conclusion.	My writing does not develop a central idea and there are not enough details.	• Sentences are incomplete, and they are not varied. • My writing has many errors in grammar, spelling, capitalization and punctuation.

Name _____

My Goals

In this module, you will write an expository essay. An expository essay explains or informs the reader about a topic.

Think about your writing. What do you think you do well as a writer? How might you like to improve? Add your own goals to the list below.

☐ Do research on my topic.

☐ Provide a clear thesis sentence.

☐ Develop the thesis with several paragraphs.

☐ Provide supporting details.

☐

☐

☐

☐

As you plan, revise, and edit your expository essay, refer to these goals to make sure you are meeting them.

Name _____

Planning Chart

Complete the following chart to help you plan your expository essay.

Prompt (Write the prompt in this column.)	Topics (Write the topics that interest you, and circle the one you choose.)	Thesis Statement (Write one or two statements that help focus your topic.)	Research (Write facts and details from your research.)

Now it is your turn to begin research on your topic. Keep your research notes on this page or in your notebook.

Name _____

Expository Essay

A Silly Invention

1   In 1943, James Wright, an engineer who was working hard to invent a new substance for the Unites States government, had a failure that turned into a happy accident. He and his team had been working day and night trying to make a substance that could substitute for natural rubber. The government needed this new substance for jet engines. It had to be strong enough to tolerate hot jet engines and cold weather.

2   After a full year of hard work, Wright and his team came up with a putty that was a failure. It was gooey and not at all what they needed. Wright threw it on the floor. To his surprise, it bounced. Soon, Wright discovered that the putty had other interesting properties. It could stretch. When pressed onto a newspaper or comic book, it could pick up images.

3   A businessman named Peter Hodgson named the substance "silly putty," put it in a plastic egg, and sold it to the public. Silly putty soon became a popular toy for kids. Eventually, people saw that silly putty could be useful too. People with hand injuries began using it to increase hand strength. Adults used it for removing lint from fabric and stabilizing rickety furniture. It was even used by Apollo 8 astronauts to keep their tools in place when they went to the moon.

4   Wright's hard work may have seemed like a failure at first, but, in fact, his invention provided hours of fun for generations of children. Silly putty also served important and useful purposes that he never imagined while creating it. His silly invention turned out to be seriously amazing.

Organizing Your Essay

Use the chart to plan the organization of your essay. Don't worry about making your writing perfect at this point. Just get some ideas down.

Introduction • Introduce the topic. • Include a thesis statement. • Get the reader's attention.	
Body Develop the topic with any of the following— • facts • definitions • concrete details • quotations • examples	
Conclusion Provide a concluding statement that is related to the thesis.	

Peer Proofreading

Use this checklist as you proofread.

- ☐ Is there a name on the paper?
- ☐ Check for correct use of the verbs *be* and *have*.
- ☐ Check for correct use of all other verbs.
- ☐ Check for correct use of verb tense.
- ☐ Check whether irregular past-tense verbs are written correctly.
- ☐ Check for correct subject-verb agreement.
- ☐ Check for proper punctuation.

Name _____

Revisit Your Goals

How Did I Do? Congratulations! You finished your expository essay. Look at the goals you set on page 1.3. Did you meet them? What could you do better with your next piece of writing? Write two or three sentences to tell how you think you did.

_____

_____

_____

_____

_____

_____

_____

_____

_____

_____

_____

_____

Name _____

Word Bank

As you listen to *The Mesmer Menace*, jot down any interesting words, phrases, or sentences. Use this Word Bank as a resource while you draft and revise your writing.

Story

A Noise in the Night

<u>I tried not to think about</u> the time I heard a strange noise coming from the wall that separated my room from Matt's. I remember working at my desk late one night when I heard what sounded like marbles dropping on the tile floor. "Matt? Is that you?" I called again, "Matt?" No answer.

Name _____

My Goals

In this module, you are going to write a narrative. A narrative can be a fictional story in any kind of genre or subgenre.

Think about stories you have read. What did you like about them? What made them interesting to you? What kind of stories do you like? On the lines below, add goals of your own.

☐ Write a story in the genre I have chosen.

☐ Use descriptive details for the setting and characters.

☐ Include dialogue.

☐ Narrate the events of the plot, or conflict.

☐

☐

☐

☐

As you plan, draft, revise, and edit your narrative, look back at this list of goals to make sure you are meeting them.

Name _____

Story Rubric

Use this rubric to develop and revise your draft story. Try to score a 4 in each category!

	Organization	Ideas & Support	Conventions
Score 4	My story is crafted with purposeful structure, includes plot elements, and uses literary devices.	My writing develops an engaging plot with details—including characters, setting, and dialogue.	• My sentence structure and word choice contribute to the clarity of my story. • My writing includes proper grammar, spelling, capitalization, and punctuation.
Score 3	My story has a structure, includes most plot elements, and uses some literary devices.	My writing develops a plot with specific details—including characters and setting.	• My sentence structure and word choice mostly contribute to the clarity of my story. • My writing has a few errors in grammar, spelling, capitalization or punctuation.
Score 2	My use of plot elements and literary devices is not effective. There is some structure.	My writing has a weak plot with few details.	• My sentence structure and word choice may weaken my story. • My writing has errors in grammar, spelling, capitalization, and punctuation.
Score 1	My story has little structure, uses no literary devices, and the narrative is hard to follow.	My writing does not develop a plot and includes very few details.	• My sentence structure and word choice do not contribute to the clarity of my story. • My writing has many errors in grammar, spelling, capitalization and punctuation.

Freewriting

Use the space below to continue developing your story.

What is your sentence frame?

_____

Complete the sentence frame and continue the freewrite.

_____

_____

_____

_____

_____

Elements of Narrative From your freewrite, begin to develop your story by identifying the narrative elements.

Setting

_____

Characters

_____

_____

Possible events for plot

_____

_____

_____

Story

Inside the Box

1   <u>Lying on the ground, still as a dead chicken, I looked up.</u>

2   *Thump-thump.*

3   The ground was cold, dark, and damp. There appeared to be a box covering my entire body from head to toe. I could smell the wood above me and the moist soil beneath me.

4   My arms lay cramped beside me. *Can I move them? My legs. Can I feel them?* I jerked my arms up toward the boards above me to push away the wood. I couldn't reach. My breath got heavier, my eyes widened, and my fear began to grow.

5   "Where am I?" I asked myself again. Nobody could hear me—at least not in this box. Was the box keeping me in or keeping something out?

6   I jerked my legs up to see if they could reach the top of the box. Success! My feet reached a board above my chest, and with one quick motion, I pushed with all my might. A board creaked, and dust fell on my face; no luck. I thought about how I used to lie on the bottom bunk and push my legs up to bump my brother's top bunk from underneath. I loved to push hard enough to annoy him but gently enough not to break the boards.

7   These boards, however, needed to break. I pushed again twice as hard and twice as long, and the board moved an inch—maybe two—before returning to its original position. A waterfall of dust fell through the wooden boards and onto my face and chest, choking me for a moment and causing my eyes to burn. I coughed. I rubbed my eyes. My fear began to turn into panic.

8   Without warning, I heard a door slam. It was close. Real close. I paused, held my breath, and listened.

9   *Thump-thump*.

10   One thing was very clear: I had to get out—and soon.

Write your conclusion to this model in your notebook before writing the conclusion to your own story.

Name _____

Characterization Chart

4. Actions	3. Inner Qualities	2. Description	1. Name

8. Reactions	7. Comparisons	6. Impact	5. Dialogue

Name _____

Revisit Your Goals

How Did I Do? Well done! You finished your story. Look at the goals you set on page 2.3. Did you meet them? What could you do to meet your goals with your **next** piece of writing? Write two or three sentences that tell how you think you did.

_____

_____

_____

_____

_____

_____

_____

_____

_____

_____

_____

_____

Name _____ *mary*

Predictions and Questions About
Green City

Use this sheet to make predictions and ask questions about *Green City*.

I predict that the setting of this book will be

about Natural Disaster

I predict that the characters in this book will be

will organize

What will the story be about?

Beginning: _She the natural_

disaster

Middle: _biulding_

End: _happy_

The parts that are fiction may be _____

_____

The facts I will learn may be about _____

_____

Questions I have about this book are:

1. _____

2. _____

3. _____

Name _____

Clarifying Questions

Use this sheet to clarify the three questions about *Green City* that you generated on page 3.1.

Your questions:

_____

_____

_____

_____

Can the questions be made clearer? If so, revise them.

_____

_____

_____

_____

_____

Can the questions be made more specific? If so, revise them.

_____

_____

_____

_____

Name _____

Responding to Green City

Answer the questions about *Green City* to analyze the author's argument.

What is the **issue** that the townspeople disagree on in *Green City*? _____

_____

_____

What is the author's **position** on the issue? _____

_____

_____

What are the **arguments** in favor of the author's position? _____

_____

_____

_____

What are **arguments** against the author's position? _____

_____

_____

_____

Did the book change how **you feel**? Explain. _____

_____

_____

_____

Name _____ Matt _____

Word Bank

Jot down interesting words and phrases that the author of *Green City* uses to describe natural disasters. Then come up with some of your own words to describe natural disasters, cleaning up, relocating, and rebuilding. Use this Word Bank as a resource as you draft and revise your writing.

government rubble future
tornado sustainable
gigantic
immediately
flood approaching
destroyed
thousands
shredded

Name _____

Pros and Cons of Rebuilding

Use this chart to list the pros and cons of rebuilding versus moving away.

Rebuilding Pros	Rebuilding Cons
biulding grew/school no home work	working haerd biulding more paper
Moving Away Pros	**Moving Away Cons**
im taking my mony so i dont get hert	leaving friends and mom dad and big bro

My Position: If a tornado destroyed My city I would stay and biuld

Persuasive Essay Rubric

Use this rubric to develop and revise your persuasive essay. Challenge yourself to get a 4 in each category!

	Organization	Ideas & Support	Conventions
Score 4	My writing is skillfully organized, with a purposeful structure, around a clear central point of view.	My writing clearly supports a central point of view with strong facts, reasons, and other evidence.	• My sentence structure and word choice contribute to the clarity of my essay. • My writing includes proper use of grammar, capitalization, punctuation, and spelling.
Score 3	My writing is organized around a clear central point of view and has a structure.	My writing supports a central point of view with some facts, reasons, and other evidence.	• My sentence structure and word choice mostly contribute to the clarity of my essay. • My writing has a few errors in grammar, capitalization, punctuation, and spelling.
Score 2	My writing is organized with some structure. The central point of view may be weak or unclear.	My writing weakly supports a central point of view. Evidence may be too brief or unrelated to my point of view.	• My sentence structure and word choice may not contribute to the clarity of my essay. • My writing has errors in grammar, capitalization, punctuation, and spelling.
Score 1	My writing may not be organized. The central point of view may be missing or unclear.	My writing does not use evidence to support a central point of view.	• My sentence structure and word choice do not contribute to the clarity of my essay. • My writing has many errors in grammar, capitalization, punctuation, and spelling.

Name _____

My Goals

In this module, you will write a persuasive essay about whether to rebuild or move away if a natural disaster strikes.

Think about your past writing. What did you do well? What do you want to improve about your writing? Add your own goals to this list.

- ☐ Introduce my topic with a clear statement of opinion.

- ☐ Provide at least three reasons that support the opinion.

- ☐ Support each reason with facts, details, and examples.

- ☐ Use transitional words, phrases, and clauses to connect ideas.

- ☐ Use persuasive language.

- ☐ Provide a concluding statement giving my opinion.

- ☐ Organize the essay in a way that is logical.

- ☐

- ☐

- ☐

- ☐

- ☐

Persuasive Essay

1   Would the threat of a volcanic eruption make you move? Most readers would probably say, "Yes, of course!" However, I am quite certain that for my family the answer is no. We will continue to stay in our home even though we live under the constant threat of evacuation because of an active volcano nearby. It can be scary to think that we may have to leave if the lava starts to flow this way and that all of our things may be destroyed. Regardless, we have many compelling reasons to stay exactly where we are.

2   Most importantly, we have an abundance of history in our home. My great-grandfather built our house with his bare hands. That means I am the fourth generation of my family that has lived in our home. Each generation has left a mark by building additional rooms, adding new roofs, and planting trees. My sister and I painted a mural on the wall of our bedroom this year. We would not want to leave a home so filled with our own personal history.

3   Additionally, we have deep roots in our community. Our neighbors, like us, have decided to stay despite the volcanic threats. We are very close to our neighbors. Every Saturday, we spend the afternoon discussing community issues. Then, we all share a meal, and the kids talk until the adults make us go to bed. How could we bear to leave such great friends?

Name _____

4   Moreover, we will never find another town with as much natural beauty as our town. We love the sounds and smells of the ocean. In the summer, all the kids in our town play on the beach. We also work together on projects to keep the beach clean and free of litter. Even the volcano is a beautiful sight, despite its sometimes ominous presence.

5   Obviously, starting again somewhere else would be very difficult for my family. We would have to say goodbye to our beloved home, our wonderful community, and our beautiful town. We would be forced to live in a strange house and in a community of strangers. When weighed against the possibility of a volcanic eruption, the scales tip heavily toward staying here. We know that if the lava begins to flow this way, we will get a warning and we will have to quickly leave. At that point, we risk losing everything. But, for now, we are here, safe in our beloved home.

Name _____

Research Organizer

This graphic organizer will serve as your research plan. Identify the facts and details that BEST support your argument. Put a star next to each of those details. You will use them in your persuasive essay.

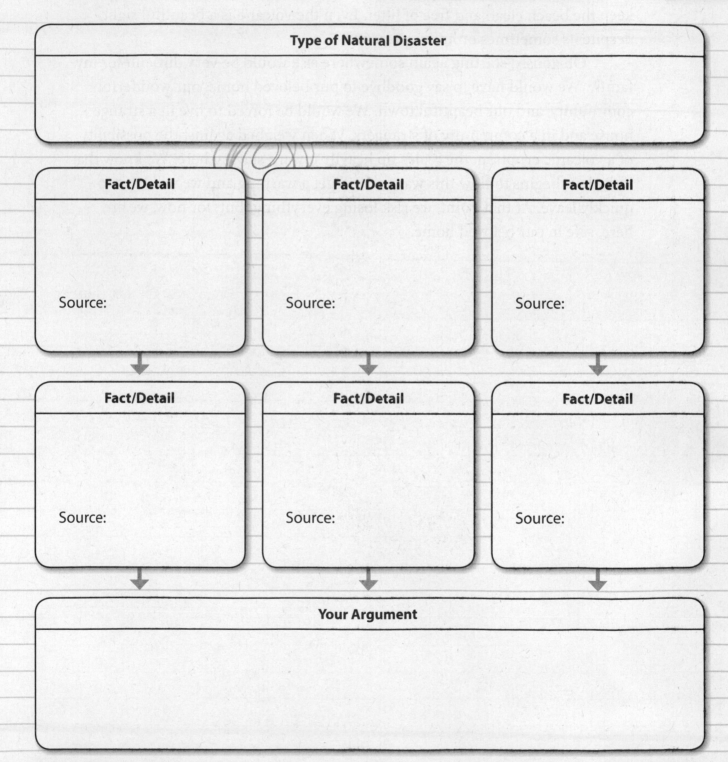

Type of Natural Disaster

Fact/Detail	**Fact/Detail**	**Fact/Detail**
Source:	Source:	Source:

Fact/Detail	**Fact/Detail**	**Fact/Detail**
Source:	Source:	Source:

Your Argument

Name _____

List of Sources: Bibliography

Record this information for any **books** you gather information from.

Author's Last Name, First Name. <u>Book Title</u>. Publisher location: Publisher, Copyright date.

_____

_____

_____

_____

Record this information for any **websites** you gather information from.

Last Name, First Name (if known). "Article/Website Title." <u>www.url.com</u>, Date accessed.

_____

_____

_____

Record this information for any **magazines** you gather information from.

Last Name, First Name. "Article Title." <u>Magazine Title</u>, Date of issue. p. 00.

_____

_____

_____

Name _____

Persuasive and Transitional Words and Phrases

Consider using the following words in your persuasive essay. Add your own words to the list.

- certain / sure / good / correct

- scientific / researched / proven

- true / accurate / precise

_____

_____

_____

Consider using the following transitions in your persuasive essay. Add your own words to the list.

- on the other hand / at the same time / however

_____

_____

_____

Clocking Checklist

1. Editor: _____

Is there a **name** on the paper? _____

2. Editor: _____

Are there any **sentence fragments** to correct? _____

_____

3. Editor: _____

Are there any **run-on sentences** to correct? _____

_____

4. Editor: _____

Do all sentences and proper nouns start with a **capital letter**? _____

_____

5. Editor: _____

Do all sentences have correct **subject-verb agreement**? _____

_____

6. Editor: _____

Do all sentences have **proper punctuation**? _____

_____

7. Editor: _____

Are there any **spelling** errors? _____

Name _____

Revisit Your Goals

How Did I Do? Well done! You finished your persuasive essay. Look at the goals you set on page 3.7. Did you meet them? What could you do to meet your goals with your next piece of writing? Write two or three sentences that tell how you think you did. Be sure to think about and write at least two new goals.

_____

_____

_____

_____

_____

_____

_____

_____

_____

_____

_____

_____

Name _____

Questions About Traveling West

What questions do you have about traveling west in the 1850s? Write at least one of each of the following question types: *WHO, WHAT, WHERE, WHEN, HOW*. Then, write any other questions that you have.

WHO who is the guy with you?

_____

WHAT what dose the horse look like?

_____

WHERE where are you going ?

_____

WHEN when did you sleep?

_____

HOW how fare did you go?

_____

Other Questions Did you eat?
What did you do when you were there.

_____

_____

_____

Name _____

Word Bank

Jot down interesting words and phrases from *On the Santa Fe Trail*. Use this Word Bank as a resource as you draft and revise your letter requesting information.

Name _____

Letter Rubric

Use this rubric to develop and revise the draft of your letter. Check your letter to make sure it meets the top descriptions here and go for a 4 in each category!

	Organization	Ideas & Support	Conventions
Score 4	My letter is skillfully organized around a main idea. It includes an introduction, transitions, and a conclusion.	My letter includes a clear request for information with a formal greeting and closing.	• The sentences in my letter are varied, and word choices are specific and clear. • My writing includes proper grammar, usage, capitalization, punctuation, and spelling.
Score 3	My letter is mostly organized around a main idea. I have an introduction, a conclusion, and some transitions.	My letter includes a mostly clear request for information and includes a greeting and closing.	• The sentences in my letter are mostly varied, and the word choices are mostly specific and clear. • My writing has a few errors in grammar, usage, capitalization, punctuation, and spelling.
Score 2	My letter has some organization. I may be missing an introduction, a conclusion, or some transitions.	My letter may include a request for information but may not include a greeting and closing.	• The sentences in my letter may be awkward and not varied. • Few words are specific. • My writing has more than a few errors in grammar, usage, capitalization, punctuation, and spelling.
Score 1	My letter may not be organized. It may not include an introduction, transitions, or a conclusion.	My letter may not include a request for information or a greeting and closing.	• There is no variety of sentences in my letter. • Some sentences are incomplete. • No words are specific. • My writing has many errors in grammar, usage, capitalization, punctuation, or spelling.

Name _____

My Goals

In this module, you are going to write a letter to a museum or a historical society to request information about traveling west in the 1850s.

Think about your past writing. What did you do well? What do you want to improve with your writing? Add your own goals on the lines below.

☐ Introduce myself.

☐ Explain the letter's purpose.

☐ Include the following required parts of a formal letter—

heading	body
date	closing
salutation	signature

☐ Use details to request specific information.

☐ Use formal language.

☐

☐

☐

☐

☐

Use these goals as a checklist to develop your letter draft into a focused piece of writing.

Formal Letter

March 25, 2020 ⎤ Date

Sanchez Elementary School ⎤
1111 South Street   Heading
El Paso, Texas 79901 ⎦

National Trails Intermountain Region ⎤
Santa Fe National Historic Trail
PO Box 728   Inside Address
Santa Fe, NM 87504 ⎦

To Whom It May Concern: ⎤ Greeting

1   I am a student in the fifth grade at Sanchez Elementary School. We are studying westward expansion. We have read Marion Russell's experiences *Along the Santa Fe Trail*. It is a story about a young girl's experiences on a wagon train in 1852. However, I would like more information about the conditions for other children after they left Missouri and were on their way to New Mexico. I will use the information to complete a class project on the topic.

2   Would you please send me any materials that you have about the conditions along the trail? I would like to receive maps of the journey through the five states and information or films about interesting sites along the way. I would also like to read other firsthand accounts of people who were children traveling along the Santa Fe Trail. Would you please provide me with a list of titles and authors?

Body

Name _____

3

In addition, I would like to know answers to the following questions:

- How many wagon trains traveled along the trail in a year?
- How did the children attend school while they were traveling?
- What chores did the children have?

4

I am very interested in the lives of children on wagon trains heading west, which is why I am requesting several types of information and materials to help me. If you could answer my letter as soon as possible and send any information and materials you can, I would certainly appreciate it.

Body

Sincerely,] Closing

Diego Hernandez] Signature

Name _____

Letter Organizer: Parts of a Letter

Use the following letter organizer to plan and write a draft of your formal letter.

Date _____

Heading _____

_____

_____

Inside Address _____

_____

_____

Greeting _____ :

Body _____

_____

_____

_____

_____

_____

_____

_____

Closing _____ ,

Signature _____

Name _____

Improve Word Choice by Deleting Ideas

Read the following sentences. Which ideas need to be deleted to improve the word choice of the sentences? Mark through phrases and sentences that can be deleted. Rewrite the improved sentence in the space provided.

1. My idea is to ask a museum to please send me information about the buffaloes that travelers could see along the Santa Fe Trail, such as how many there were.

   _____

   _____

   _____

2. I am writing a letter to you. My letter is about the diseases that travelers might suffer. Please send information about the travelers along the Santa Fe Trail. I heard that cholera was a disease. Were there many others?

   _____

   _____

   _____

3. One idea I had was to write about the buffalo. But I have never seen a buffalo. I have never seen a buffalo wallow. I would like to see a picture of a buffalo wallow someday. Oh, by the way, would you please send me a picture?

   _____

   _____

   _____

Name _____

Editing

1. Editor: _____

Is there a **name** on the paper? _____

2. Editor: _____

Are there any **sentence fragments**? _____

_____

3. Editor: _____

Are there any **run-on sentences**? _____

_____

4. Editor: _____

Do all sentences start with a **capital letter**? _____

_____

5. Editor: _____

Do all sentences have correct **subject-verb agreement**? _____

_____

6. Editor: _____

Do all sentences have **proper punctuation**? Are words **spelled correctly**?

_____

7. Editor: _____

Do the **salutation** and the **closing** use **proper punctuation**? ___

_____

Name _____

Revisit Your Goals

How Did I Do? Well done! You finished your formal letter requesting information. Look at the goals you set on page 4.1. Did you meet them? What could you do to meet your goals with your next piece of writing? Write two or three sentences that tell how you think you did. Be sure to think about and write at least two new goals.

_____

_____

_____

_____

_____

_____

_____

_____

_____

_____

_____

Name _____

Word Bank

As you review *The Elephant Keeper* and work on writing an editorial, jot down interesting words and phrases you come across. You can use this Word Bank as a resource as you draft and revise your writing.

Name _____

Editorial Rubric

Use this rubric to develop and revise your draft editorial. Make sure you have facts to back up your claim. Proofread your writing carefully and go for a 4 in each category!

	Organization	Ideas & Support	Conventions
Score 4	My editorial is skillfully organized around a central claim. It has an introduction, transitions, and a conclusion.	My editorial defends my central claim with facts, reasons, and other evidence.	• My sentence structure and word choice contribute to the clarity of my editorial. • My writing includes proper use of grammar, capitalization, punctuation, and spelling.
Score 3	My editorial is organized around a central claim. It has an introduction, transitions, and a conclusion.	My editorial mostly defends my central claim with facts, reasons, and other evidence.	• My sentence structure and word choice mostly contribute to the clarity of my editorial. • My writing has a few errors in grammar, capitalization, punctuation, and spelling.
Score 2	My editorial has some structure. The central claim may be unclear. It may be missing an introduction, a conclusion, or transitions.	My editorial weakly defends my central claim. My evidence may be too brief or unrelated to my claim.	• My sentence structure may be awkward, and there may be little variety. • My word choice may be vague. • My writing has errors in grammar, capitalization, punctuation, and spelling.
Score 1	My editorial may not be organized. The central claim may be missing or unclear.	My editorial may not defend a central claim. Evidence is too weak. My central claim may be missing or unclear.	• My sentence structure and word choice do not contribute to the clarity of my editorial. • My writing has many errors in grammar, capitalization, punctuation, and spelling.

My Goals

You are going to write an editorial. An editorial is meant to persuade readers to think or act in a certain way.

Think about your past writing. What did you do well? What do you want to improve as you write an editorial? What will you need to do in order to write a successful editorial? Add your own goals to the lines below.

☐ Clearly state my central idea about an environmental issue.

☐ Provide specific support for the idea.

☐ Write clear, coherent sentences.

☐

☐

☐

☐

Use these goals as a checklist to develop your editorial draft into a focused piece of writing.

5.3

Name _____

Developing a Plan

Write your environmental topic in the chart. Next, write your position on the topic. Then write facts you already know that support your position.

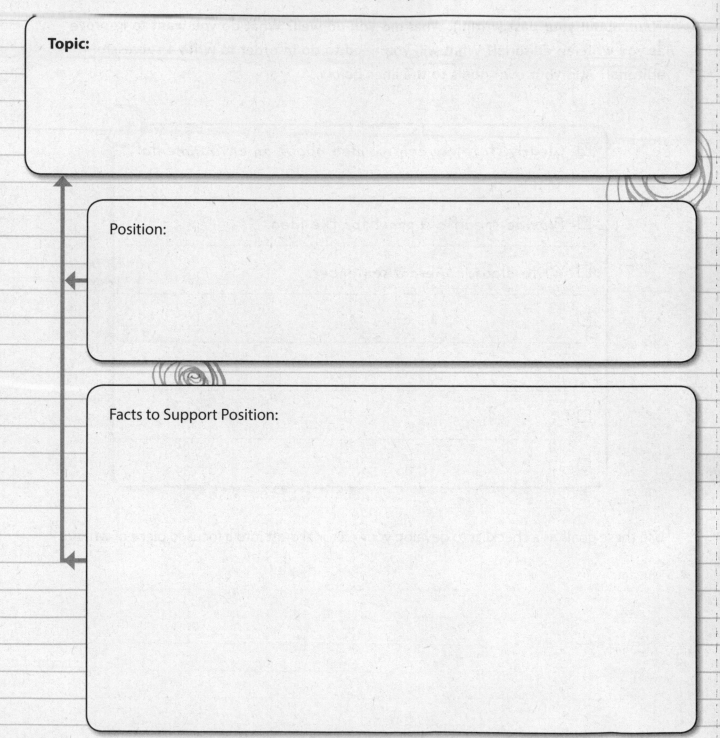

Topic:

Position:

Facts to Support Position:

Name _____

Editorial

What About Water Bottles?
by Stella Grise

1   As I leave soccer practice, I toss my empty water bottle into the recycling can. I do the same after a game. Sometimes the can is so full that empty bottles spill out and blow away. I started to think about all those bottles. After learning from <u>NewsTime</u> magazine that Americans drink billions of gallons of water from plastic bottles each year, I formed a new opinion. Sports teams should require athletes to use reusable water bottles.

2   Players I talked to had reasons for using disposable bottles. It's fast and easy just to grab a bottle of water. They like the taste of the bottled water. Besides, used bottles can be recycled, and just one bottle wouldn't make a difference.

3   These are silly reasons. It's easy to grab a prefilled bottle, but how much time does it take to fill a reusable bottle? I timed this at home. Getting a bottle ready took less than a minute. That's hardly any time at all!

4   I did an experiment on how water tastes. I chilled both kinds of water overnight, and then I gave ten friends drinks to see if they could tell the difference. Most people could not taste any difference. Only one person said she could tell, but she incorrectly said that tap water was bottled water because it "tasted better"!

5   Saying water bottles can be recycled is correct, but the Bottled Water Council reports that just a third of all bottles are recycled. In addition, plastic bottles are made of oil. The bottles are filled in a plant that uses fuel. More fuel is used to transport the bottles to stores. These uses of fuel cause pollution.

6   The last reason, that "one bottle doesn't make a difference," is just an excuse. According to Marcus Grant, author of Water: Our Most Precious Resource, it actually takes about three liters of water to make one liter of bottled water! We all must do whatever we can to use resources wisely. Teams should step in to help people change their habits. If athletes used reusable bottles, that would make a big difference. Please ask your team to make a rule to use reusable bottles.

_____

Sources

Aaron, Ava. "Americans Turn to Bottled Water." NewsTime, March 10, 2018. pp. 23–24.

"Bottled Water." www.thebottledwatercouncil.example.com. May 14, 2018.

Grant, Marcus. Water: Our Most Precious Resource. Dallas, TX: Fresh Water Press, 2015.

Name _____

Developing Inquiry Questions

Answer these questions to help you gather information to support your position.

1. What is a broad question about my topic?

_____

_____

2. How can I clarify the question, or make it more focused?

_____

_____

3. What questions should my research focus on?

_____

_____

_____

_____

Name _____

Gathering Information from Sources

List the sources you use for facts in your editorial and tell why you know each source is credible. Then restate the information you will use to demonstrate you understand it.

Primary Sources		
Title	**I know it's credible because**	**Information I will use**

Secondary Sources		
Title	**I know it's credible because**	**Information I will use**

Name _____

Plagiarism and Paraphrasing

Tell whether each statement should be credited to a source. Explain why or why not.

1. It takes me about ten minutes to ride my bike to school.

_____

2. Our city adds 3 tons of garbage to the landfill every day.

_____

3. After sunset, owls and other creatures come out.

_____

4. Limiting the amount of trash put in the landfill will make the landfill last longer.

_____

Suppose you want to use the following information from a website in an editorial. Paraphrase it. Be sure you demonstrate an understanding of the information by restating it accurately.

Plastics in the aquatic environment are of increasing concern because of their persistence and effect on the environment, wildlife, and human health.

_____

_____

_____

Name _____

Revising Checklist

Use this checklist to help you revise your editorial.

Did I—

Use the genre characteristics of an argumentative text by

☐ including a thesis statement?

☐ giving supporting reasons?

☐ using facts to back up my reasons?

Use the craft involved in writing an argumentative text by

☐ writing coherent sentences?

☐ writing clear sentences?

☐ elaborating with descriptive details?

☐ choosing words carefully?

Name _____

Revisit Your Goals

How Did I Do? Congratulations! You finished your editorial. Look at the goals you set on page 5.3. Did you meet them? What could you do better with your next piece of writing? Write two or three sentences that tell how you think you did.

_____

_____

_____

_____

_____

_____

_____

_____

_____

_____

_____

_____

_____

Name _____

Word Bank

Jot down any interesting words and phrases you hear or read. You can use this Word Bank as a resource as you draft and revise your writing.

Brainstorming Quicklist

Use the chart to brainstorm ideas for your personal narrative. In the first column, quickly write names of family, friends, pets, places, and things. Add descriptions to the second column. In the third column, jot down brief memories related to the items in the first column.

Names	Descriptions	Anecdotes
⭐ Jay	wedgie Toy story	I'll never forget when . . . he rifed my underware
mom		I'll never forget when . . .
dad		I'll never forget when . . .
Tiago		I'll never forget when . . .
ms soza		I'll never forget when . . .

My Goals

In this module, you will write a personal narrative about an experience you will never forget.

Think about your past writing. What did you do well? What can you do to improve your writing? Add your own goals on the lines below.

- ☐ Write a strong opening sentence that hooks the reader.
- ☐ Use vivid words to help readers share the experience.
- ☐ Use different kinds of sentences to make my writing more interesting.
- ☐ use punswashin
- ☐
- ☐
- ☐

As you plan, draft, revise, and edit your personal narrative, turn back to these goals to make sure you are meeting them.

Name _____

Personal Narrative Rubric

Use this rubric to develop and revise your draft personal narrative. Remember that only you can tell your story, so challenge yourself to score a 4 in each category.

	Organization	Ideas & Support	Conventions
Score 4	My narrative tells a personal story with memorable events in the order they took place.	My writing develops an engaging plot, using concrete and vivid words and sensory language.	• My sentence structure and word choice contribute to the clarity of my story. • My writing includes proper grammar, spelling, capitalization, and punctuation.
Score 3	My narrative tells a personal story with events in the order they took place.	My writing develops a plot, using some concrete and vivid words and some sensory language.	• My sentence structure and word choice mostly contribute to the clarity of my story. • My writing has a few errors in grammar, spelling, capitalization, or punctuation.
Score 2	My narrative includes some personal memories, but they may not be in order.	My writing has some structure and uses a few concrete or vivid words with little sensory language.	• My sentence structure and word choice may weaken the clarity of my story. • My writing has errors in grammar, spelling, capitalization, or punctuation.
Score 1	My narrative includes a few memories, and they are not in order.	My writing does not develop a plot and uses very few concrete or vivid words or sensory language.	• My sentence structure and word choice do not contribute to the clarity of my story. • My writing has many errors in grammar, spelling, capitalization, and punctuation.

Name _____

Personal Narrative

The Ship of the Desert

1   The endless sea of sand glittered in the dazzling sunlight as our trusty vehicle bounced merrily across the landscape. My friends and I chattered excitedly as we spotted our destination. Men in vivid blue robes and eye-popping orange turbans waited patiently beside animals I had only seen in movies or the zoo. I pinched myself to prove this was real. It was! Thousands of miles from home, I was going to ride a camel in the Sahara of Morocco!

2   I had pictured sitting in a cushy saddle between two humps, but that bubble quickly burst. These were dromedaries—camels with only one hump right in the middle of their backs. The hump was thickly padded with colorful blankets, and the saddle was perched on the very top—tied on with ropes! Yeah, that seems safe!

3   As I gingerly approached the camel, it was kind enough to lie down. Whew! I didn't need a ladder to get to the saddle. Fully expecting the camel to object, I swung my leg over the saddle, grabbed the T-shaped metal bar and held on for dear life! Good thing, because when a camel stands up, it's like getting whiplash on a crazy carnival ride!

4

Once we were "all aboard" our camels, we began our ride up and down the steep sand dunes. I soon understood why camels are called "ships of the desert." When they walk, they rock and roll like a boat on a stormy sea. Was I going to get seasick in the middle of the desert? Forget that! I was having the time of my life—dreaming that I was part of an ancient camel train carrying exotic spices across the sands to distant lands.

5

Too soon, the ride was over, but not really. I will never forget the magical experience of being a passenger on a ship of the desert.

Name _____

Revisit Your Goals

How Did I Do? Well done! You finished your story. Look at the goals you set on page 6.3. Did you meet them? What could you do to meet your goals with your next piece of writing? Write two or three sentences that tell how you think you did.

_____

_____

_____

_____

_____

_____

_____

_____

_____

_____

_____

_____

_____

Name _____

Word Bank

As you listen to *The Day-Glo Brothers* and learn about writing a research report, jot down any interesting words and phrases. You can use the Word Bank as a resource as you draft and revise your research report.

Name _____

K-W Chart

In the chart below, write what you already know about your topic. Then write questions you have about the topic that will help guide your research.

Topic	
What I KNOW	**What I WANT to Know**

Name _____

My Goals

In this module, you are going to write a research report about an invention that has impacted your life.

Think about your past writing. What did you do well? How can you improve your writing? Add your own goals on the lines below.

- ☐ Use facts and data.
- ☐ Write an opening that draws the reader into the report.
- ☐ Ask questions as I research the topic.
- ☐
- ☐
- ☐
- ☐
- ☐

As you plan, draft, revise, and edit your research report, turn back to these goals to make sure you are meeting them.

Name _____

Research Report Rubric

Use this rubric to develop and revise your research report draft. Reach to score a 4 in each category!

	Organization	Ideas & Support	Conventions
Score 4	My report is skillfully organized around a main idea with an introduction, a conclusion, and transitions.	My report develops an engaging main idea and includes specific details, in my own words, using the research I did.	• My report uses a variety of sentence structures. • My word choice contributes to the clarity of my report. • My report includes proper grammar, capitalization, punctuation, and spelling.
Score 3	My report is mostly organized around a main idea with an introduction, a conclusion, and some transitions.	My report mostly develops one main idea with specific details from my research.	• My writing uses some variety in sentence structures. • My word choice usually contributes to the clarity of my report. • My writing has a few errors in grammar, capitalization, punctuation, and spelling.
Score 2	My report may have a weak organization and an unclear main idea with no introduction, conclusion, or transitions.	My report hardly develops a main idea. It has few details from my research.	• Few of my sentences are varied. • My words may be general and do not contribute to the clarity of my report. • My writing has some errors in grammar, capitalization, punctuation, and spelling.
Score 1	My report may have a missing or unclear main idea. It may not include an introduction, conclusion, or transitions.	My report does not develop a main idea, and there are not enough details.	• My sentences are not varied. • My word choice does not contribute to the clarity of the report. • My writing has many errors in grammar, capitalization, punctuation, and spelling.

Research Report

The First Mobile Phone

1   The year was 1973. Martin Cooper was walking in New York and could barely hold his excitement. He was about to announce to the world what he had invented: the first cell phone—a phone that could be carried anywhere and wasn't attached to a wall or copper wires.

2   But first, he stopped on the street and thought he might make a call. Did he think about calling his wife? His mother? His boss? No, he called a man at Bell Labs, a company that had bragged that they would invent the first cell phone. He dialed, and Joel Engel answered. Traffic whizzed by and people stared. Martin said casually, "I'm calling you from a cell phone—a real cell phone—a personal hand-held cell phone."

3   However, this first cell phone was nothing like the sleek phones we use today. It weighed 28 ounces, which is like carrying a jumbo-sized can of tomatoes. Most phones today have batteries that last over a day, while the first cell phone's battery only lasted 30 to 60 minutes. Oh, and that first phone had a large rubber and wire antenna, large enough to nudge a cat off a couch. Another huge difference was the price. It cost around $4,000! (Keith, 2004)

4   It wasn't perfect, but the first cell phone paved the way for an electronic revolution. Some people have done away with their in-home landlines and only use cell phones. Fifty years ago, people could only dream about talking on a cell phone at a ball game or at a swimming pool. Today, cell phones are everywhere!

Name _____

Track Your Sources

For each book, magazine, or website you use, keep a list here or in your notebook. Keep this information in your shoebox.

1. Author's name (if available) _____

    Name of source (book, magazine, or website) and URL if it is a website

    _____

2. Author's name (if available) _____

    Name of source (book, magazine, or website) and URL if it is a website

    _____

3. Author's name (if available) _____

    Name of source (book, magazine, or website) and URL if it is a website

    _____

4. Author's name (if available) _____

    Name of source (book, magazine, or website) and URL if it is a website

    _____

When creating your bibliography, you will need additional information. For books, you will need the copyright date, publisher city, publisher name, and page numbers. For websites, you will need the name of the article (if available) and the day you accessed the website. For magazines, you will need the name of the magazine, the name of the article, page numbers, and the date it was published.

Name _____

Credible or Not Credible?

Use the chart below to evaluate your sources.

Source	Is it credible?	Why or why not?
1.		
2.		
3.		
4.		

Demonstrate Understanding

Go back into your drafts and use this checklist to demonstrate you understand the information you have researched.

You can demonstrate an understanding of researched information by

☐ relating your experience to the information.

☐ analyzing what you read.

☐ incorporating what you already know about a subject into the research.

☐ summarizing what you have read in your own words.

☐ drawing conclusions about what you read.

Avoid Plagiarizing

Review your drafts for places you did not give credit to your source. When you find examples of plagiarism, rewrite the text in your own words, use quotation marks, or give credit to the writer.

You are plagiarizing if you

☐ copy a source's work word for word.

☐ use a source's words or ideas without giving that source credit.

☐ do not use quotation marks in a direct quotation.

☐ copy a sentence and simply substitute a few words to make it sound original.

Name _____

Questions to Ask

Ask your conferencing group the following questions, and record the feedback from your peers.

1. Do I have enough information? _____
If not, what should I add?

_____

_____

2. Do I have too much information? _____
If so, what should I cut?

_____

_____

3. Does my research report follow a logical flow? _____
If not, what should I change?

_____

_____

4. Is there anything you don't understand? _____
If so, how can I make it clearer?

_____

_____

Name _____

Editing Checklist

Check for each grammar element one at a time throughout your report.

☐ Where can I add adverbs to describe the action?

☐ Where can I add adverbs to tell when something happens?

☐ Does each pronoun agree with its subject?

☐ Do the prepositions and prepositional phrases show where something takes place or how something is done?

Clocking Checklist

Use this list as you edit one another's reports.

1. Are proper nouns and the first word in each sentence capitalized?

_____

2. Are the main words in the titles of articles capitalized?

_____

3. Are quotation marks used to signal a person's exact words?

_____

4. Is correct punctuation used at the end of each sentence?

_____

5. Are commas correctly used within sentences?

_____

6. Do pronouns agree with the subject?

_____

7. Are words spelled correctly?

_____

8. Are there complete sentences?

_____

Name _____

Bibliography

In your shoebox, separate your source types: books, magazines, websites, and encyclopedias. Use the formats on this page as a model for your bibliography.

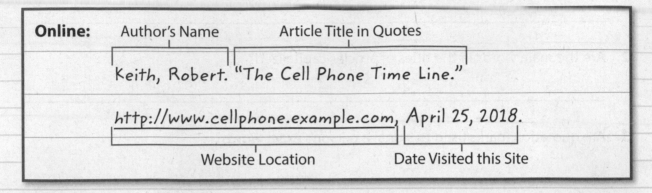

Online: Author's Name   Article Title in Quotes

Keith, Robert. "The Cell Phone Time Line."

http://www.cellphone.example.com, April 25, 2018.

Website Location   Date Visited this Site

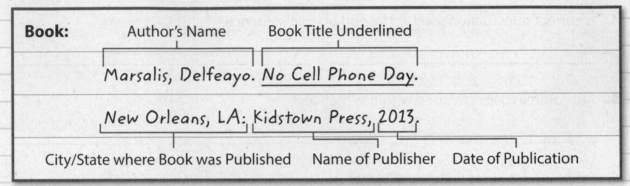

Book: Author's Name   Book Title Underlined

Marsalis, Delfeayo. No Cell Phone Day.

New Orleans, LA: Kidstown Press, 2013.

City/State where Book was Published   Name of Publisher   Date of Publication

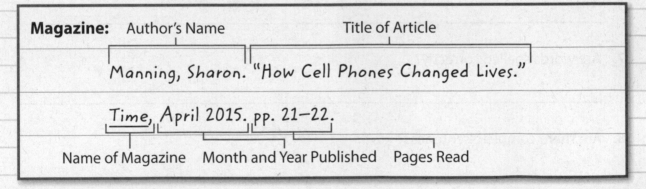

Magazine: Author's Name   Title of Article

Manning, Sharon. "How Cell Phones Changed Lives."

Time, April 2015. pp. 21–22.

Name of Magazine   Month and Year Published   Pages Read

Encyclopedia:

Name of Reference Book   Number of Edition   Title of Article

Encyclopedia Britannica: 16th Ed., "Mobile Telephones."

Name _____

Revisit Your Goals

How Did I Do? Congratulations! You finished your research report. Look at the goals you set on page 7.3. Did you meet them? What could you do better when you write your next research report? Write two or three sentences that tell how you think you did.

_____

_____

_____

_____

_____

_____

_____

_____

_____

_____

_____

_____

Name _____

Word Bank

As you listen to *Love That Dog* and learn about poetry, jot down any interesting words and phrases. You can use the Word Bank as a resource as you draft and revise your poem.

Lyric Poem Rubric

Use this rubric to develop and revise your draft lyric poem. It will help guide you to write the best lyric poem you can. Make it your goal to score straight 4s!

Score	Organization	Ideas & Support	Conventions
4	My writing skillfully uses the elements of poetry within a structure that fits the poem.	My writing develops an engaging idea and uses figurative language, such as metaphor and simile.	• My sentence structure and word choice contribute to the success of my poem. • My writing includes proper grammar, spelling, capitalization, and punctuation to fit the poem.
3	My writing uses the elements of poetry within a structure that mostly fits the poem.	My writing mostly develops an engaging idea and uses some figurative language, such as metaphor and simile.	• My sentence structure and word choice mostly contribute to the success of my poem. • My writing has a few errors in grammar, spelling, capitalization or punctuation.
2	My writing may use some elements of poetry within some structure, but it may not be right for the poem.	My writing may develop an idea but uses little figurative language, such as metaphor and simile.	• My sentence structure and word choice may not contribute to the success of my poem. • My writing has errors in grammar, spelling, capitalization, or punctuation.
1	My writing uses no elements of poetry, and its structure may not be right for a poem.	My writing does not develop an idea and uses no figurative language, such as metaphor and simile.	• My sentence structure and word choice do not contribute to the success of my poem. • My writing has many errors in grammar, spelling, capitalization and punctuation.

Name _____

My Goals

In this module, you will write a lyric poem describing a place you love to be, a place where you feel very at home.

Think about the times you have written poetry in the past. What did you do well? What can you do to improve your writing? Add your own goals on the lines below.

☐ Make sure my poem expresses a feeling.

☐ Write in lines and stanzas.

☐ Use descriptive language.

☐

☐

☐

☐

☐

As you plan, draft, revise, and edit your poem, turn back to these goals to make sure you are meeting them.

Name _____

Writing Metaphors and Similes

Similes and metaphors are ways of describing things. You are writing about the idea that "home is where the heart is," so you want to describe a place that is very dear to you. It could be a home, but it could also be a place where you feel completely at home. Where do you feel completely at home?

Similes

To write a simile about a home, think of a quality that a home has. Then think of something else that has that quality and write a phrase about it, beginning with *like* or *as*. The first one is done for you.

Quality that a home has:	A simile about another thing with that quality:
solid	*as a fortress*

_____   _____

_____   _____

_____   _____

_____   _____

Metaphors

Metaphors often use "to be" verbs, such as *was*, *were*, and *are*. They may also use words figuratively, as in this example: *My mother flew up the stairs.* Try creating some metaphors or changing your similes into metaphors by removing *like* or *as*.

Our house was a fortress.

_____

_____

_____

Name _____

Expanding a Line

What idea do you want your poem to focus on?

_____

Which line or lines that you have written best present that idea?

_____

Time to play with words! Use the space below to change or improve the line or record ideas that will expand on the idea in the line. One idea will spark another, so write down whatever occurs to you. Use the best lines for your poem.

Revising to Use Descriptive Words

Replace boring words in the poem with vivid verbs and adjectives.
Choose words that help create a mood.

The Blue Bird
The blue bird sits
upon

the dry round brown
nest

on the dark black
branch

near the green
leaves.

8.6

Name _____

Conferencing

Feedback Use these questions as you discuss your poem. Take notes as you receive feedback from members of your group. Then use the feedback to revise your poem.

- How does the poem reflect the idea that "home is where the heart is"?

- Do the lines and stanzas break in logical places?

- Could the poet add any graphic elements?

- Did the poet use onomatopoeia or alliteration? If so, where? Could any be added?

- Did the poet include similes or metaphors? If so, where? Could any be added?

- Are there any words that could be replaced with more descriptive words? Which ones?

Name _____

Revisit Your Goals

How did I do? Congratulations! You finished your lyric poem. Look at the goals you set on page 8.3. Did you meet them? What could you do better with your next piece of writing? Write two or three sentences about how you think you did.

_____

_____

_____

_____

_____

_____

_____

_____

_____

_____

_____

_____

_____

Characters in *The Egypt Game*

Use this chart to record what you learn about Melanie and April.

What I know about Melanie	How do I know?	What I know about April	How do I know?

Name _____

Word Bank

Jot down interesting words and phrases that the author of *The Egypt Game* uses to describe Melanie and April in the chapter "Enter Melanie and Marshall." Use this Word Bank as a resource as you draft and revise your writing.

Name _____

Descriptive Words

Fill in each box with descriptive words and phrases. Be creative!

HOW _____ **LOOKS:**

HOW _____ **ACTS:**

OTHER WORDS ABOUT _____ **:**

Name _____

Imaginative Story Rubric

Use this rubric to develop and revise your draft imaginative story. It can help you tackle the problems you encounter in your writing and come out with straight 4s.

	Organization	Ideas & Support	Conventions
Score 4	My story is crafted with purposeful narrative structure and moves logically through plot elements.	My writing develops an engaging plot with specific details, including characters, setting, and dialogue.	• My sentence structure and word choice contribute to the clarity of my story. • My writing includes proper grammar, spelling, capitalization, and punctuation.
Score 3	My story has a narrative structure and moves through most plot elements.	My writing develops a plot with specific details, including characters and setting.	• My sentence structure and word choice mostly contribute to the clarity of my story. • My writing has a few errors in grammar, spelling, capitalization, or punctuation.
Score 2	My use of narrative structure may be weak. My story uses some elements of plot.	My writing does not develop a strong plot and contains few details.	• My sentence structure and word choice may weaken the clarity of my story. • My writing may have errors in grammar, usage, capitalization, and spelling that interfere with its effectiveness.
Score 1	My story has little narrative structure and uses no narrative elements. The narrative is hard to follow.	My writing does not develop a plot and contains very few details.	• My sentence structure and word choice do not contribute to the clarity of my story. • My writing has many errors in grammar, spelling, capitalization, and punctuation.

Name _____

Freewriting Using Sentence Frames

Freewriting Rules

- **Keep your hand moving.** DO NOT stop to think.

- **Make mistakes.** DO NOT worry about spelling, punctuation, or grammar.

- **Write anything.** DO NOT worry about what others will think.

- **Keep going.** DO NOT erase, cross out, or stop writing.

1. All through the month of _____

_____

_____

_____

2. It all started when _____

_____

_____

_____

3. But in between all the good times, _____

_____

_____

_____

4. As they walked to the door, _____

_____

_____

_____

Name _____

My Goals

In this module, you are going to write an imaginative story. What are your goals for the story? Add them to the list below.

- ☐ Introduce and describe a strong main character.
- ☐ Have the character's actions drive the plot.
- ☐ Include sensory details.
- ☐ Write dialogue that has purpose.
- ☐
- ☐
- ☐
- ☐
- ☐

As you plan, revise, and edit your imaginative story, refer to these goals to make sure you are meeting them.

Imaginative Story

Never Again

1   It all started when Ting was goofing around with her little neighbor, Jorge, doing a terrible job juggling some lemons. Every time she dropped a lemon, she groaned loudly and scrambled around the shiny yellow kitchen to retrieve it, which made Jorge burst into uncontrollable giggles.

2   "Jorge is turning six next Saturday," Mrs. Garcia said. "Would you dress up as a clown and entertain his friends?"

3   "I'd love to!" Ting said, the words slipping out of her mouth like a too-loose ring slipping off a finger.

4   Ting absolutely hated wearing costumes, and she wasn't crazy about clowns. Why had she just agreed to this? But Mrs. Garcia's smile and the delight on Jorge's face made the answer clear. Ting had agreed because she couldn't bear to disappoint people that she cared about.

Name _____

5   When Saturday arrived, Ting found herself running around in the hot July sun in the Garcias' backyard. Kids were everywhere, chasing her and trying to squeeze the squeaky red clown nose Mrs. Garcia had given her. There was no shade to be found, and she was terribly hot in the red and white polka-dotted jumpsuit and crazy orange wig.

6   "Never again," Ting vowed to herself as sweat poured down her face.

7   At the end of the party, when she was dressed in her regular clothes, Ting sat down next to Ms. Ross to eat a slice of cake.

8   "I want to hire you for Lisa's party," Ms. Ross said.

9   When Ting opened her mouth to respond, she realized a yes was about to emerge. Suddenly, Ting knew what to do. She deposited a big forkful of cake into her open mouth and chewed slowly, waiting for a no to make its way to her lips.

Understanding and Naming Characters

With your group, create questions to ask about characters. Then, answer each question to create an interesting character in your imaginative story.

1. Question: _____

    Answer: _____

2. Question: _____

    Answer: _____

3. Question: _____

    Answer: _____

4. Question: _____

    Answer: _____

5. Question: _____

    Answer: _____

Character's name: _____

Character's history: _____

_____

_____

_____

Clocking

1. Editor: _____

   Is there a **name** on the paper? _____

2. Editor: _____

   Are there opening and closing **quotation marks** around **direct dialogue**?

   _____

3. Editor: _____

   Is **direct dialogue indented** for each speaker? _____

4. Editor: _____

   If **direct dialogue** is introduced by a **dialogue tag**, is the tag followed by a **comma**?

   _____

5. Editor: _____

   Are there any **sentence fragments** or **run-on sentences** that need to be corrected?

   _____

6. Editor: _____

   Do all sentences have correct **subject-verb agreement**? _____

7. Editor: _____

   Do all sentences have **correct punctuation**? _____

8. Editor: _____

   Are there any **spelling** errors? _____

Name _____

Revisit Your Goals

How Did I Do? Congratulations! You finished your imaginative story. Look at the goals you set on page 9.6. Did you meet them? What could you do better with your next piece of writing? Write two or three sentences to tell how you think you did.

_____

_____

_____

_____

_____

_____

_____

_____

_____

_____

_____

_____

_____

Name _____

Word Bank

As you listen to *The One and Only Ivan* and conduct research for your letter to the editor, jot down any interesting words and phrases you encounter. Next to the word or phrase, record the author's message. Also record any vivid verbs you want to remember. You can use this Word Bank as a resource as you draft and review your writing.

Name _____

Letter to the Editor Rubric

Use this rubric to develop and revise your draft letter to the editor. Which statements in the rubric describe your letter? Challenge yourself to score a 4 in each category!

	Organization	Ideas & Support	Conventions
Score 4	My writing is skillfully organized with a purposeful structure around a clear central claim.	My writing strongly defends a central claim with facts, reasons, and other supports.	• My sentence structure and word choice contribute to the clarity of my letter. • My writing includes proper use of grammar, capitalization, punctuation, and spelling.
Score 3	My writing is organized with a structure around a clear central claim.	My writing mostly defends a central claim with facts, reasons, and other supports.	• My sentence structure and word choice mostly contribute to the clarity of my letter. • My writing has a few errors in grammar, capitalization, punctuation, and spelling.
Score 2	My writing is organized with some structure. The central claim may be weak or unclear.	My writing weakly defends a central claim. Supports may be too brief or not related to the claim.	• My sentence structure and word choice may not contribute to the clarity of my letter. • My writing has errors in grammar, capitalization, punctuation, and spelling.
Score 1	My writing may not be organized. The central claim may be missing or unclear.	My writing may not be organized. The central claim may be missing or unclear.	• My sentence structure and word choice do not contribute to the clarity of my letter. • My writing has many errors in grammar, capitalization, punctuation, and spelling.

My Goals

In this module, you are going to write a letter to the editor. A letter to the editor shares an opinion or tries to get people to take action.

Think about your past writing. What did you do well? What do you want to do to improve your writing? Add your own goals on the lines below.

☐ Share an opinion or an idea for others to act on.

☐ Research my topic.

☐ Share facts that support my opinion or idea.

☐ Organize my letter logically.

☐ Use vivid verbs.

☐

☐

☐

☐

As you plan, draft, revise, and edit your letter, turn back to these goals to make sure you're meeting them.

Letter to the Editor

1   To the Editor:

2   I love animals. I have always wanted a pet, but my little sister is allergic to many animals. Many other families in our community are in a similar situation. Happily, our Community Pet Shelter has a program for people who love animals but cannot own one.

3   The program is called Play with Pets, or PWP. The Pet Shelter trains volunteers in how to care for and interact with the cats and dogs. Then the volunteers sign up to be at the shelter at least once a month for a three-hour session.

4   Play with Pets helps the animals a lot. Virginia Petrini, the director of the shelter, says that animals like human attention, and the shelter staff doesn't always have time to play with the animals. The animals get more exercise when volunteers play with them. The animals also get used to being around different people.

5   Play with Pets also helps people a lot. I like being a PWP volunteer. The dogs and cats are cute, and they always are happy to see me and my father when our shift begins. That makes me feel good. I think it is great that even though I am a kid, I can help the animals in our community. Even eight-year-olds can volunteer, but an adult must come with volunteers who are under 14.

6   If you love animals, think about joining PWP. It's fun and easy, and it helps our community a lot! The next volunteer training begins in two weeks, so contact the Community Pet Shelter if you are interested.

7   Respectfully,

8   David Gertz

Name _____

Conferencing

Say Back As you listen to a group member's letter to the editor a second time, take notes about what you liked or especially noticed—words, phrases, or images. Also note what you want to know more about. Then share your observations. If you run out of space, continue on another sheet of paper.

Conference Use these sentence starters to talk about each group member's draft.

> *I liked the way you . . .*

> *I'd really like to know more about . . .*

Name _____

Revisit Your Goals

How Did You Do? Congratulations! You finished your letter to the editor. Look at the goals you set on page 10.3. Did you meet them? What could you do better with your next piece of writing? Write two or three sentences that tell how you think you did.

_____

_____

_____

_____

_____

_____

_____

_____

_____

_____

_____

Time for Memories!

For each object you think of, write down all the memories, ideas, words, and phrases that come into your mind. Write down every idea you have—it might spark another idea. One of these ideas may give you an inspiration for your story.

What is your first treasured object?

What memories and emotions does it produce for you?

What is your next treasured object?

What memories and emotions does it produce for you?

What is your next treasured object?

What memories and emotions does it produce for you?

Name _____

Memory Web

As you sift through your memories, use this web graphic organizer to link one memory to another. You can also add emotions and descriptive words that your memories bring to mind. This web can be a resource for your writing.

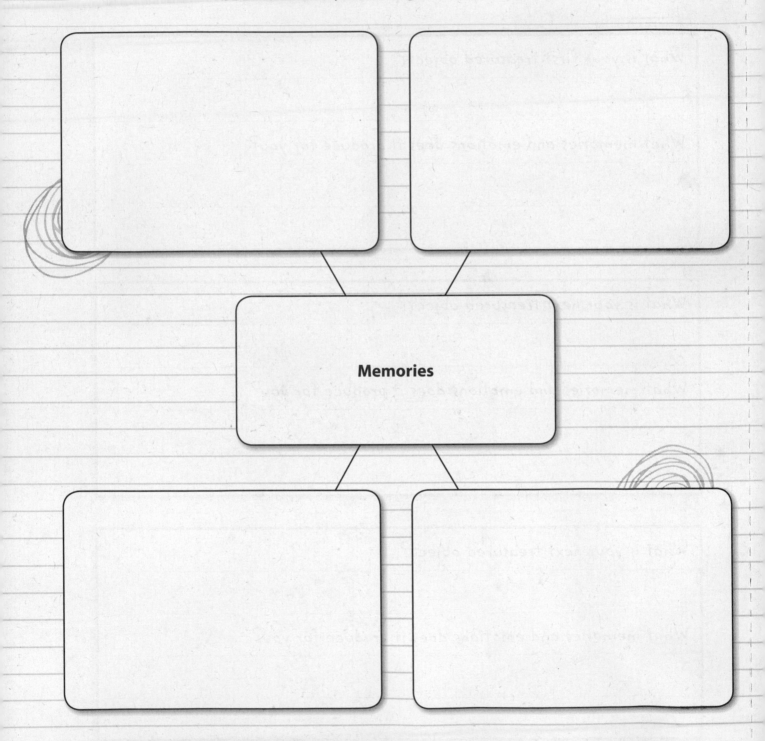

Memories

Word Bank

As you listen to *Love, Amalia* and think about your story, jot down any interesting words and phrases. You can use this Word Bank as a resource as you draft and revise your writing.

Topic Chart

Use this chart to brainstorm ideas. Write at least three ideas in each column.

People	Places	Communities

Planning

What is your topic?

_____

_____

Think About Audience and Purpose Now that you have your topic, think about who you want to read your story and your reason for writing. Note that you can have more than one purpose.

Who is my audience?

☐ family members

☐ classmates

☐ friends

☐ general public

☐ other: _____

_____

What is my purpose for writing?

☐ to entertain

☐ to inform

☐ to persuade

☐ other: _____

_____

Name _____

My Goals

In this module, you will write a realistic story that is based on a person, place, or community of people you know well.

Think about stories you have written in the past. What did you do well? What can you do to improve your writing? Add your own goals on the lines below.

☐ Write a strong opening sentence that hooks the reader.

☐ Organize with a purposeful structure.

☐ Improve word choice and sentence structure by adding, deleting, combining, and rearranging ideas.

☐ Use descriptive details for the setting and characters.

☐ Include dialogue.

☐ Use different kinds of sentences to make my writing more interesting.

☐

☐

☐

Use these goals as a checklist to develop your realistic story draft into a focused piece of writing.

Name _____

Realistic Story

The Night of the Candy Apple Disaster

1   Jessica smiled at herself in the mirror. "Yes," she thought, "I look quite nice!" She was wearing a flouncy white blouse with many ruffles and a wide, multicolored skirt that fell in tiers to below her knee. But best of all, for this night, she was wearing her mother's golden, fan-shaped earrings and her bright red lipstick. With this costume, she was SURE that she would win the Fall Fest Fashion Parade for Grade 5 at South Ward Elementary.

2   "Jessica!" her mother called. "Are you ready? Let's go or we will be late."

3   Jessica hurried to the front door and jumped in the car beside her three younger brothers—the twins, Markus and Michael, and little four-year-old Orlando.

4   Every year the Community Club sponsored a Fall Fest at the elementary school. Every room hosted games or activities, and at the end of the evening, there was a costume parade with prizes for Silliest, Scariest, and Most Creative Costumes. Jessica hoped to win Most Creative.

5   Once they arrived at the school, Jessica's mother said, "Take Orlando with you, while I go with Markus and Michael. Make sure Orlando has fun and don't lose him."

6   Jessica's heart sank. The LAST thing she wanted to do was to take care of her little brother—again. "Oh, Mom, do I HAVE to?" she whined. "He is too much trouble."

7   "Yes, Jessica. Please help. Meet me back here in an hour, and we can go to the cafeteria for the contest. And remember, don't lose Orlando."

8   Disappointed, Jessica started pulling Orlando through the halls. In one room, she played a game and won a big stuffed animal for Orlando. In another room, families were bobbing for apples. If they got an apple, they could take it to the back, where Mr. Force would dip it into the steaming red liquid to make candy apples.

9   "Apples!" Orlando cried. "I want a candy apple!"

10   Jessica sighed. With his small mouth, Orlando could not bite into the apple. "Of course, I have to do this for you," groaned Jessica.

11   She stuck her head into the bucket, bit into the apple, and carried it quickly over to Mr. Force. Then she looked around. Orlando was gone.

12   "OH, NO!" she cried. "ORLANDO! COME BACK!" She grabbed the candy apple from Mr. Force. Carrying Orlando's apple and his stuffed animal, she ran from the room and into the hall, where she fell over her little brother. He was standing by Markus and Michael, each of whom had paper cups of orange drink.

13   Down went Jessica, down went the cups full of orange drink on top of her white, ruffled blouse, and down went the bright red candy apple on her skirt. It grazed her face and left a trail of bright red, sticky candy on her cheeks. One of her mother's earrings fell off, and her lipstick was smeared.

14   "Hurry and get up, Jessica," said her mother, "or you will be late for the parade."

15   "You have got to be kidding!" Jessica cried. I won't win anything because I had to babysit my silly little brother and carry all his prizes and I fell and made this mess and everyone will laugh at me."

16   "Never mind a little inconvenience," said her mother. "The show must go on. Now get up there and act like nothing happened."

Jessica tried to make the best of it and act like she meant to look that way, but no one was fooled. However, after the parade, Mr. Wilson, the

17   principal, called out, "The Grand Prize winner for the most creative use of color and materials is Jessica, who dared to wear a white blouse splashed with orange drink and a multicolored skirt with a dash of candy apple!"

Orlando cheered loudest of all, while his big sister Jessica, who had lost

18   Orlando for just one disastrous moment, beamed at receiving her prize.

Name _____

Realistic Story Rubric

Use this rubric to develop and revise your draft realistic story. Remember to write about what is familiar to you and aim for 4s!

	Organization	Ideas & Support	Conventions
Score 4	My story is crafted with purposeful narrative structure and moves logically through plot elements.	My writing develops an engaging plot with specific details, including characters, setting, and dialogue.	• My sentence structure and word choice contribute to the clarity of my story. • My writing includes proper grammar, spelling, capitalization, and punctuation.
Score 3	My story has a narrative structure and moves through most plot elements.	My writing develops a plot with specific details, including characters and setting.	• My sentence structure and word choice mostly contribute to the clarity of my story. • My writing has a few errors in grammar, spelling, capitalization, or punctuation.
Score 2	My use of narrative structure may be weak. My story uses some elements of plot.	My writing does not develop a strong plot and contains few details.	• My sentence structure and word choice may weaken the clarity of my story. • My writing may have errors in grammar, usage, capitalization, and spelling that interfere with its effectiveness.
Score 1	My story has little narrative structure, uses no narrative elements, and is hard to follow.	My writing does not develop a plot and has very few details.	• My sentence structure and word choice do not contribute to the clarity of my story. • My writing has many errors in grammar, spelling, capitalization, and punctuation.

Name _____

Story Map

Title _____

Setting

Characters
    Protagonist:
    Other Characters:

Conflict
1. Event
2. Event
3. Event
4. Climax
5. Falling Action
Resolution

Name _____

Conferencing

Conference with a partner. As you read your partner's story, take notes on this page in the box below. Use your partner's notes to you to revise your draft to improve sentence structure and word choice.

- Does the setting, or time and place of the story, grab your attention?

- Are the characters interesting and well-rounded?

- Is the conflict in the story believable and interesting?

- What happens at the climax of the story?

- Is the conclusion of the story satisfactory?

- Did the writer use details and elaboration to make the story come alive? If so, can you point them out?

- What suggestions for improvement would you make?

Name _____

Revisit Your Goals

How Did I Do? Well done! You finished your realistic story. Look at the goals you set on page 11.6. Did you meet them? What could you do to meet your goals with your next piece of writing? Write two or three sentences that tell how you think you did. Be sure to think about and write at least two new goals.

_____

_____

_____

_____

_____

_____

_____

_____

_____

_____

_____

Word Bank

As you listen to *Words with Wings* and learn about narrative poetry, jot down any interesting words and phrases. You can use the Word Bank as a resource as you draft and revise your poem.

Name _____

Narrative Poem Rubric

Use this rubric to develop and revise your narrative poem. As you write your story in the form of a poem, challenge yourself to score a 4 in each category!

	Organization	Ideas & Support	Conventions
Score 4	My writing skillfully uses the elements of poetry within a narrative structure to tell a story.	My poem develops an engaging story and uses sensory details, figurative language, and specific words.	• My sentence structure and word choice contribute to the clarity of my poem. • My writing includes proper grammar, spelling, capitalization, and punctuation to fit the poem.
Score 3	My writing uses some elements of poetry within a narrative structure that mostly tells a story.	My poem develops a story and uses some sensory details, figurative language, and specific words.	• My sentence structure and word choice mostly contribute to the clarity of my poem. • My writing has a few errors in grammar, spelling, capitalization, or punctuation.
Score 2	My writing may use some elements of poetry within some structure, but it may not be right for a narrative poem.	My poem may develop a story but uses few sensory details, a little figurative language, and general words.	• My sentence structure and word choice may not contribute to the clarity of my poem. • My writing has errors in grammar, spelling, capitalization, or punctuation.
Score 1	My writing uses no elements of poetry, and it does not tell a story.	My poem does not develop a story and uses no sensory details, figurative language, or specific words.	• My sentence structure and word choice do not contribute to the clarity of my poem. • My writing has many errors in grammar, spelling, capitalization, and punctuation.

My Goals

In this module, you will write a narrative poem that tells a story from your life's experiences.

Think about a time you have written poetry in the past. What did you do well? What can you do to improve your writing? Then think about when you wrote a story with a beginning, a middle, and an end. What did you enjoy about writing it? How can you improve on your storytelling? Add your own goals on the lines below.

☐ Make sure my poem tells a story.

☐ Make sure my poem has a beginning, a middle, and an ending.

☐ Use figurative language.

☐

☐

☐

☐

As you plan, draft, revise, and edit your narrative poem, turn back to these goals to make sure you are meeting them.

Narrative Poem

Ruffed Grouse in Snow

Snow on snow
Brittle winds blow
A grouse takes cover
Burrowing
  down
     in
       a
         den
           of
             snow.

1

My snowshoes touch the ground,
I try not to make a sound.
Still, my footsteps do pound,
And a grouse awakes inside her hidden mound.
And flies

2

                  sight!
              of
            out
        soaring
     Soaring,

Story Map

Use this story map to plan your narrative poem.

Beginning

Middle

Ending

Name _____

Write a Conclusion

Think about the main point of your poem. Write it in the box below.

My Main Point

Now think about ways to end your poem. Write one idea in each box below. Then choose one idea to use in your poem.

1.

2.

3.

4.

Narrative Poem

My Stuff, His Stuff

1
My brother Hal borrows my stuff
My scarf, my gloves, my soccer ball.
When we get on the bus,
I notice he's got it all.

2
I decide to trick him so I
Hide everything under the bed.
He doesn't fall for that,
And raids my closet instead.

3
I give up and say, Go ahead!
You can have my soccer shoe,
My hat, my football, and gloves
But watch out!
I'm going to take your stuff, too.

4
It's odd.
My brother no longer takes my things,
After he missed his video game.
Now he leaves my stuff alone
And I respect his just the same.

Name _____

Clocking

Your classmates will record their comments about your narrative poem here.
Use their notes to make corrections.

Items to check:

- capitalization of proper nouns and the first word in each line

- correct use of punctuation within and at the end of lines

- correct spelling

- unclear or vague words

- other comments

This page belongs to _____.

1. _____

   _____

2. _____

   _____

3. _____

   _____

4. _____

   _____

5. _____

   _____

Name _____

Revisit Your Goals

How Did I Do? Congratulations! You finished your narrative poem. Look at the goals you set on page 12.3. Did you meet them? What could you do better when you write your next narrative poem? Write two or three sentences that tell how you think you did.

_____

_____

_____

_____

_____

_____

_____

_____

_____

_____

_____